OPTICAL ILLUSIONS

Page 4
High divers in Palm
Springs, California
during the opening
ceremony for the
El Mirador swimming
pool in 1929. High diver
Dutch Smith seems to
have thrown his diving
partner Georgia
Coleman high into the
air; in fact, she jumped
from a higher spring-
board. Perfect timing!

This is a Parragon Publishing book

Copyright © Parragon Books Ltd

Parragon Books Ltd
Queen Street House
4 Queen Street
Bath BA1 1HE, UK

Layout: Sabine Vonderstein, Cologne
Picture acquisition: Barbara Linz, Cologne
Concept and production: Nazire Ergün, Cologne

English edition produced by: APE Int'l, Richmond, VA
Translation from German: Markus Flatscher for APE Int'l

ISBN 978-1-4054-9571-4

Printed in Indonesia

The works of Salvador Dalí © Salvador Dalí, Gala-Salvador Dalí Foundation/VG
Bild-Kunst, Bonn 2007

WARNING: Some of the illustrations contained in this book may cause dizziness and
disorientation when viewed for extended periods of time. The publisher is not liable
for any damage incurred from viewing the contents of this book.

OPTICAL ILLUSIONS

AMAZING DECEPTIVE IMAGES—WHERE SEEING IS BELIEVING

INGA MENKHOFF

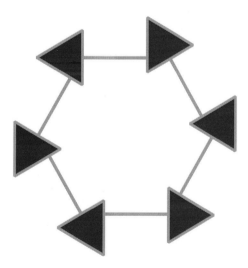

Bath · New York · Singapore · Hong Kong · Cologne · Delhi · Melbourne

CONTENTS

VISUAL PERCEPTION

Pictures may say a thousand words—but do they always tell the truth? Human perception is primarily visual perception: no other sensory organ processes more information for us than our eyes. Our eyes enable us to see what surrounds us; however, the image we perceive does not always match reality. Sometimes we perceive spaces, objects, movements, pictures or colors that do not exist, or we misjudge the length or size of objects. Examples of tricks of the eyes are legion, and they occur in various forms—their common root lies in our system of visual perception. Even when we are aware that our eyes are playing a trick on us, it can be nearly impossible to correct the wrong perception.

Mural paintings in Pompeii, dating back to the 1st century CE. Pompeiian artists often exploited optical illusion, and fictive architecture was especially popular.

VISUAL PERCEPTION
AN (ALMOST) PERFECT CHOREOGRAPHY OF EYES AND BRAIN

An impressive church dome? Actually, this is an illusion: the dome does not exist. The Italian painter and architect Andrea Pozzo created this perfect optical trick in the Roman church of Sant'Ignazio in the 17th century by creating sophisticated distortions of perspective.

In Rome, a traveler steps inside the Baroque church of Sant'Ignazio. He strides through the church, overwhelmed by the lavish decoration, when he notices a mark on the floor. He stops and raises his eyes. To his amazement, he now sees a massive dome above. How can that be? He had thoroughly studied the church from outside before entering, and there was definitely no sign of any dome! Later, our traveler leafs through a magazine over an espresso in a small café. An advertisement catches his eye. Suddenly, the letters seem to detach themselves from the page and flow in a wave-like motion. How is that possible? In the evening, the visitor settles down on a terrace in a small village outside Rome. He watches the setting sun for a long time. The closer the sun gets to the horizon, the bigger it seems to become. The traveler knows this is caused by the curvature of the Earth, yet the sun actually appears to be expanding.

A church dome that appears from nowhere, moving letters in a magazine, the growing sun—our traveler has seen all these things with his own eyes, yet none of them is real. These three examples serve to show that human perception is not perfect. To understand how these illusions are caused and when they occur, it is important to know some basic facts about our sensory system.

Of all the sensory organs humans have at their disposal, the eyes have by far the highest capacity for gathering information. Unlike many animals, humans specialize in visual perception, processing some 80 percent of their total information intake visually. Millions of infinitesimally tiny receptors are a crucial component in processing visual stimuli. There are some 130 million located on the retina, connected via mediators to nerve fibers and bundled into the optic nerve. Just at the spot where the optic nerve exits the eye toward the cerebral cortex, there is a tiny area, just 2 mm (0.07 inches) across, that has no receptors. This "blind spot" is the cause of some astonishing visual illusions.

The effect can be illustrated by the black-and-white playing cards depicted at the top of the opposite page. Bring the picture close to your eyes. Cover your right eye and focus on the right card with your left eye. Now slowly move the picture away, concentrating on the right card. You will realize that at a distance of approximately 10 inches, the flowers on the left card are no longer visible.

What is happening? At a distance of approximately 10 inches—the exact distance varies from one person to another—the left picture will hit the retina's blind spot. Since this area lacks receptors that are sensitive to light, the flowers are no longer perceived. Instead, we see a blank area.

In everyday life, people do not notice any restrictions caused by the blind spot. This is partly due to constant small movements and changes of perspective that occur while scanning our environment in detail. In addition, the blind spots of the left eye and the right are not exactly congruent. Finally, psychological processes ensure that any gaps are filled in by colors and shapes from surrounding areas.

But how do our eyes produce images in the first place? How does visual perception work? To put it in simple terms, seeing is a two-stage process. The first phase is chemical and physical in nature: electro-magnetic energy is absorbed by the eye, the eye's receptors transform the energy into nerve stimuli, and these are passed on to the brain through the optic nerve. These processes are very complicated and are not crucial for an understanding of visual illusions. It is the next stage that is decisive in this respect—when the optical stimuli are processed and analyzed in the cerebral cortex. This is a necessary requirement for recognizing objects. When interpreting visual stimuli, the brain falls back on experience and previously acquired knowledge while simultaneously processing information transmitted to the brain by all the other sensory organs. This does not mean, however, that a single object will be perceived in one way at all times. The setting sun is an example in point. The size of the sun does not physically change, even though our brain tells us its size varies. This is because we do not perceive objects in isolation, but in the context of their surroundings. High in the sky, there is no framework of reference, which is why the sun appears rather small. As it approaches the horizon, however, there are trees, buildings, church towers, boats or other distinctive reference points available, which make the sun appear larger.

What does the illustration on page 9 spell?
Depending on whether a person reads the vertical column or the horizontal row, the illustration either reads "12 13 14" or "A B C." Our brain processes the picture depending on the context, meaning that the process of recognition follows logical principles.

The blind spot: If you cover the right eye and focus on the right-hand image from a distance of approximately 10 inches, the image on the left disappears.

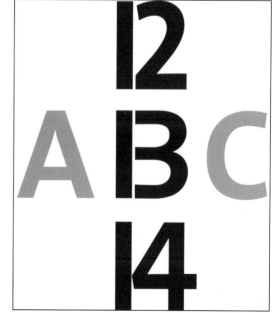

A, B, C or 12, 13, 14? This image can be read both ways.

At first glance, we see sheep grazing on a meadow. Looking at the picture more closely, we perceive something quite different.

This trompe-l'oeil painting in the Dolmabahçe Palace in Istanbul, built during the 19th century, creates the illusion of a window opening up toward the sky—a perfect illusion!

What is frolicking on this meadow?

At first sight, the photograph to the left seems unambiguous: it's a flock of sheep on a meadow, huddling close together. Upon closer inspection, however, we recognize it is something else: this is actually a group of naked people crouching on the ground, huddling next to each other. The fact that images such as this one are not part of our regular everyday experience causes our brains to misinterpret the visual signals at first.

Can you read this text?

Tihs txet is raedable eevn tuohgh the idnividaul lteters of the wrods are mxied up. The olny tihng taht mtaters is taht the frist and lsat lteters are in the rgiht plcaes. Eevrythnig esle is itnerprteed into a choernet wohle by our brian.

Even though only the first and last letters of the above words are in the correct places, we are still able to read the text with little extra effort. This demonstrates, on the one hand, that we do not perceive words as a sequence of individual letters, but as whole units. At the same time, it shows that our brains are capable of organizing unstructured information and of giving meaning to seemingly incoherent data. This process is furthered by our experience and knowledge.

Our visual perception does not always match reality. When recognizing objects, our brains must process optical stimuli, and this process is potentially faulty. Sometimes we find the illusions caused by such mistakes disturbing. Quite frequently, though, we are equally astonished and fascinated by the many forms of optical illusions.

Thus, it should come as no surprise that art and architecture have sought to exploit tricks of the eye ever since classical antiquity. A wide range of art techniques have been invented that can be grouped under the label trompe-l'oeil (French for "trick the eye"). Phantom objects appear in paintings, paintings themselves turn into phantom objects, and in other cases animals, humans and objects are represented in mural paintings and on the front of buildings so accurately that their presence and existence is never doubted by those who pass by. Notably in architecture, artists of the modern era found unlimited possibilities for expression through their rediscovery of perspective and optical illusion painting. By making sophisticated use of illusions in perspective, small rooms and short hallways have been transformed into impressive halls and seemingly endless corridors, and breath-taking ceiling frescoes make us believe that the building virtually touches the sky. Among the most popular themes in trompe-l'oeil works of art are painted windows and doors that open up to a blue sky or a green landscape, as well as gaps in walls, façades, and ceilings. These techniques create the illusion that a space contains an opening with a view of the landscape outside.

The tradition of ancient trompe-l'oeil works of art has been continued and expanded upon to this day, and has been varied with amazing results, not least with the help of electronic media. The following chapters examine the exciting and extremely diverse world of optical illusions in greater depth.

Detail of the ceiling of Villa Barbaro (16th century). High above, a window seems to open up a view of the blue sky.

A modern example of an illusion painting on the façade of a building in New York City. The painting creates the illusion of Brooklyn Bridge in the distance, seemingly located behind an extensive driveway leading up to the building.

DISTORTION ILLUSIONS

Some optical illusions trick our perception only once; as soon as we have figured out the picture's secret, we cannot be deceived a second time. Examples of this kind of illusion include puzzle pictures and ambiguous shapes (these will be presented in one of the following chapters). The majority of optical illusions, however, continue to mislead us again and again. Even when we realize that we are looking at an illusion, we are frequently not able to correct our mistaken perception. A wide range of geometric shapes, for example, make us see things that do not exist in reality: we misjudge distances, see curvatures where there are only straight lines, and perceive two-dimensional figures as three-dimensional objects. These examples are about distortions. Sometimes they affect our interpretation of length or size, sometimes of the entire shape.

Waterfalls in the city? A well-known whisky manufacturer thought up something special to advertise its product. This painting, which creates the illusion of a three-dimensional object through strong distortion of perspective, was created by pavement artists Manfred Stader and Edgar Müller in a shopping mall in Taiwan.

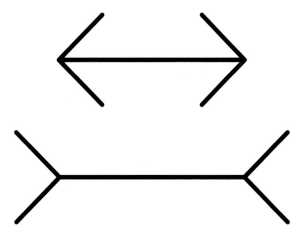

Which horizontal line is longer?

The answer is deceptively simple: we think that the lower line is significantly longer than the upper one. But beware—this is an example of our senses playing tricks on us. The illusion is caused by the angles. In the case of converging angles, the line segment appears to be shorter. A line between diverging angles, on the other hand, is perceived as being longer. This optical illusion is one of the best-known distorted distance phenomena. It was identified by Franz Müller-Lyer toward the end of the nineteenth century, hence its name, the Müller-Lyer illusion.

Which segment is longer, A–B or B–C?

In both illustrations, the segment A–B is equal in length to the segment B–C. These variants of the Müller-Lyer illusion demonstrate that we misjudge distances even when the angles are set next to each other along the same line, and when the points of the arrows are represented as filled triangles.

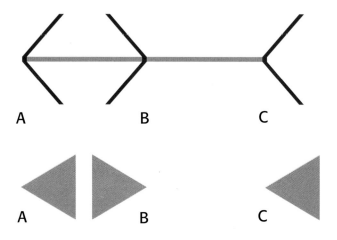

Is the red point located on the line's midpoint or to the left of it?

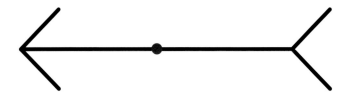

Although our impression of the matter is different, the red dot actually does divide the line into two equal segments. Subjects asked to mark the midpoint of the line almost invariably place it too far to the right, usually by as much as 20 to 30 percent.

Which horizontal line is shorter?

Both trained and untrained subjects incorrectly assess the left line as shorter than the right one. In fact, their lengths are equal. This illustration is an impressive demonstration of our propensity to perceive objects—in this case horizontal lines— in their context. While the circles cause a seeming shortening of the red line in the figure on the left, the circles placed at the ends of the line in the right-hand picture make us think the line on the right is longer.

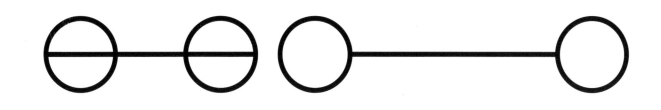

Take a look at both red lines.
How much longer is the red line to the rear compared to the red line toward the front?

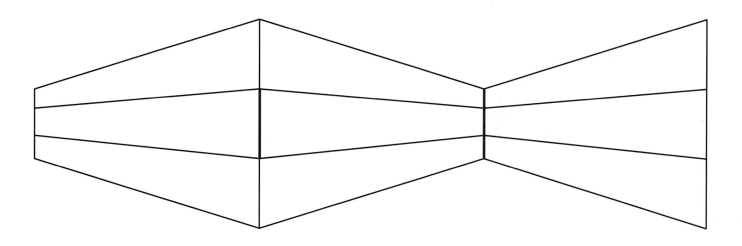

In this case, it may actually be necessary to measure the lines to convince yourself that the line further back truly is the same length as the forward line. This illustration demonstrates another variant of the Müller-Lyer illusion: what we perceive as converging (in case of the line toward the front) and diverging angles (in case of the line to the rear). The illustration also involves a trick of perspective over which we have no control.

Which of the two yellow lines is longer?

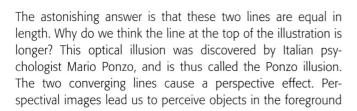

The astonishing answer is that these two lines are equal in length. Why do we think the line at the top of the illustration is longer? This optical illusion was discovered by Italian psychologist Mario Ponzo, and is thus called the Ponzo illusion. The two converging lines cause a perspective effect. Perspectival images lead us to perceive objects in the foreground as being nearer to us and those in the background as further away, because we know from experience that an object will appear smaller the further away it is. Conversely, as in this example of two lines of equal length, the line segment that appears to be further away will appear to be longer.

Which line is shorter, the red or the yellow?

There has been a lot of research that confirms that people tend to overestimate the length of vertical lines by 20 to 30 percent. Even though most people know that the sides of a triangle are longer than its height (represented by the red line in the illustration), we still tend to perceive the yellow line as being shorter. Confirming the length by measurement shows that the red line and the yellow line are of equal length.

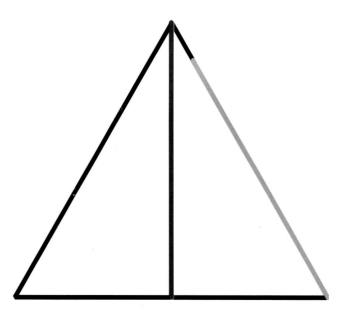

Are the red lines equally long?

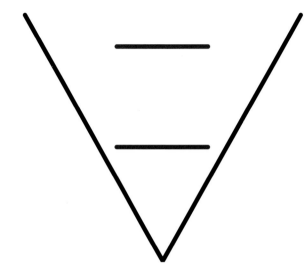

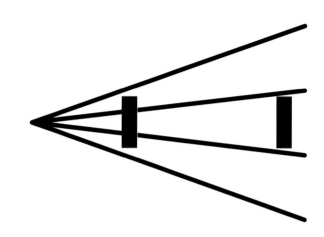

These two variants of the Ponzo illusion also demonstrate that we perceive lines that are closer to the vanishing point (the angles formed by the converging lines in the illustration) as being longer, because we interpret them as being further away. When checking their actual lengths, we are surprised to find that the red lines and red bars respectively are of equal length.

Which figure is bigger?

In the case of representations of a tunnel, the impression of depth is even stronger than in the other variants of the Ponzo illusion we have seen so far, which are based solely on converging lines. Our experience of seeing things in perspective—that objects appear smaller the further away they are—leads to a false perception. These two figures that appear to be of different sizes—the one at the back seems to be bigger—are actually identical.

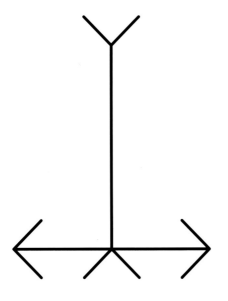

Which line is longer, the vertical one or the horizontal?

Did you choose the vertical one? If so, you are in good company: most people think that this line is longer, even though in reality, both lines are of equal length. Over-estimating heights is a characteristic human tendency. In this example, the effect of the illusion is made even more dramatic by the angles at the ends of each line segment (cf. the Müller-Lyer illusions discussed on page 14).

Which of these two rectangles is a square?

A

B

The great majority of people will say figure A is a square. The correct answer, however, is B. This is another impressive demonstration of how human beings tend to overestimate the length of vertical lines.

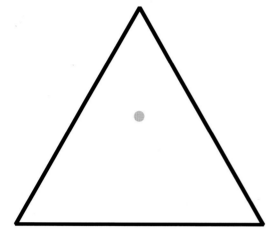

Is the dot in the upper half of the triangle or in its center?

This is another example demonstrating how we overestimate heights. We think that the point is located significantly above the center. In fact, it bisects the triangle's height exactly. The effect is compounded by another factor: the surface area below the point is much larger than the surface area above. Our brain associates the larger area with greater length.

Which line is longer: the top of trapezoid A or the top of trapezoid B?

We perceive the upper side of trapezoid A as longer. This phenomenon is caused by two factors. On the one hand, the sides end in an obtuse angle (greater than 90°), while the sides of trapezoid B end in an acute angle (less than 90°). This form of the illusion is similar to Müller-Lyer illusions, which involve the perception of line segments surrounded by converging angles as shorter and segments surrounded by diverging angles as longer. Moreover, the difference in the trapezoids' surface areas leads us to perceive the lengths of the upper sides as being different while, in fact, both lines are of equal length.

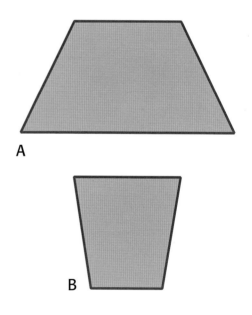

Which red line is longer?

Our perception of objects in the context of their environment, and the resultant phenomenon of falsely perceiving their dimensions, can also be demonstrated by Sander's parallelogram. The red lines are of equal length, but the context of the different areas makes them appear to be unequal. Our brain processes this picture as follows: the smaller an object in its context, the smaller its individual parts—which is a mistake, as illustrated by this example.

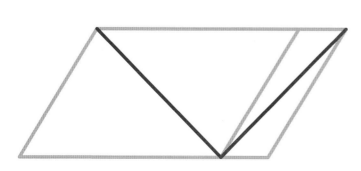

Which dimension of the Gateway Arch is greater, its height or its width?

Gateway Arch, designed by the renowned Finnish-American architect Eero Saarinen for the city of Saint Louis, Missouri, is an unmistakable and popular symbol of the city. At the same time, it is a particularly clear and impressive example of an optical illusion. Even though the steel arch's height and its width at the base both measure exactly 630 ft, we tend to overestimate the structure's height—a common, everyday mistake. Scientists believe that humans do a better job of estimating horizontal distances because our eyes are aligned on a horizontal axis, making sideways eye movements easier. Vertical eye movement, on the other hand, requires more effort on the part of the eye muscles, which in turn leads to our typical overestimation of heights.

Which of the stone elements of the Parthenon have perfect right-angles?

Very few. The characteristics of human perception that lead us to perceive buildings as either static or lively were not unknown to the ancient architects, and were taken into account in the planning of big buildings. The Athenian Parthenon, built some 2,500 years ago, is a nice demonstration of the architects' efforts to give the observer an impression of perfect harmony. This aim required sophisticated structural techniques: the Parthenon's horizontal structural elements, for instance, are expanded slightly by a few inches, although this is imperceptible to the naked eye. The curvature balances out the rigidity of the horizontal axes. The vertical elements, on the other hand, lean slightly inward, and the columns bulge somewhat.

What do you see in this image? Curved bars?

No matter how we interpret the vertical lines, the amazing fact is that none of them are curved! Apparently, the surface segments of different colors (or shades) trigger a visual stimulus that is misinterpreted by our brain, leading to the perception that we are looking at curved bars. This illusion does not occur when the lines consist of a single color throughout.

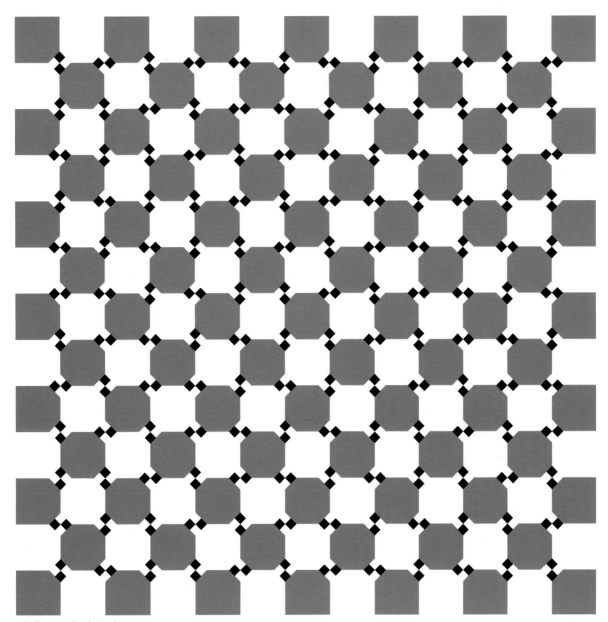

Boli of Bugs © Akiyoshi Kitaoka

Are the square surfaces of this checkered pattern parallel?

You think not? Do you think the surfaces are curved or arranged unsystematically? If so, take a ruler and convince yourself of the fact that both the horizontal and the vertical lines are straight and parallel to each other. The small black and white squares arranged between the green and white fields according to a specific scheme cause us to falsely perceive curves.

What is the angle between the red lines?

The red lines are running in straight vertical paths and are perfectly parallel. The alternating blue and green diagonal lines, however, make us believe that the vertical lines lean toward each other to varying degrees. This particular kind of parallel illusion was discovered in the 1860s by the German astrophysicist Johann Karl Friedrich Zöllner, and is called the Zöllner illusion.

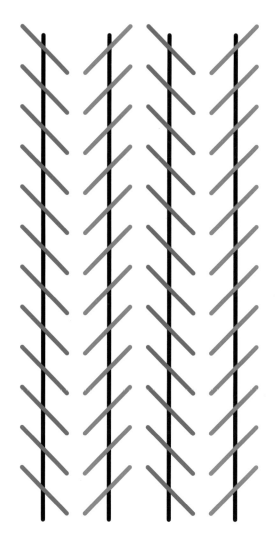

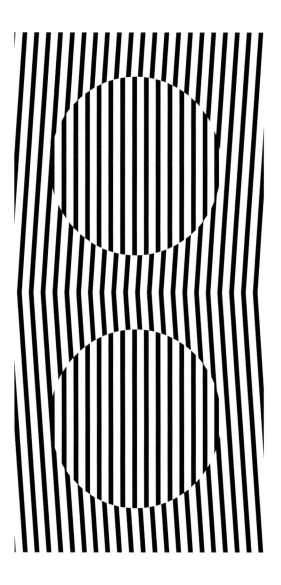

In which direction are the lines inside the circles leaning?

The answer to this question is: these lines are not inclined at all. This illusion, which was first published by Colin Blackmore, is caused by the diagonal surrounding lines. In an attempt to reconcile the conflicting visual stimuli, our brain processes the visual information so as to suggest that the lines inside the circles are leaning in the opposite direction. This is why we perceive an inclination to the left in the upper circle and an inclination to the right in the lower circle.

Where are the red lines curved to the greatest extent?

The red lines do not curve at all—they are perfectly parallel. This parallel illusion bears the name of Ewald Hering, who identified it in 1861. It is based on the human brain's propensity to perceive straight lines as being curved when they are seen against a background of radiating lines whose focal point is between the parallel lines. The impression of curvature in the red lines is strongest around the focal points of the radiating lines.

What shapes are the colored fields?

Do you perceive the colored fields as wedge-shaped? Most people do, even though they are perfectly parallel to each other. This is known as the café wall illusion. The small photograph illustrates how it came by its name: it shows the façade of a café in Bristol, England, where the black and white tile pattern creates (unintentionally, in this case) this kind of optical illusion. The café wall illusion is another type of parallel illusion.

Which square is larger?

Do you think the upper square is clearly the bigger one? If so, you have been influenced by the height of the shape. In this illustration, the upper shape is taller. Our brain automatically interprets the taller shape as having a greater surface area. In fact, the sides of the two squares are exactly the same length. The illusion disappears, by the way, when you rotate the page by about 45°.

Which arc has the strongest curvature?

This illusion is quite astonishing: we perceive the bottom arc as having the least curvature and the top one as having the most. As soon as we cover the ends of the middle and upper arcs so that all three segments are equal in length, however, we realize that the three arcs have the same curvature. This example illustrates that our assessment of curvature is strongly influenced by the length of the curved line.

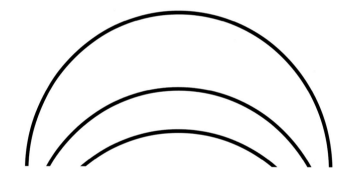

Which square appears bigger, and which heavier?

This illustration demonstrates the influence of color on perception: dark colors feel heavier than light ones. In terms of size, however, it is the other way around: light objects against a dark background appear bigger than dark objects against a light background. The cause for this illusion seems to be that the impression of light an object leaves on the retina is expanded in a way that makes light surfaces exceed their actual boundaries. This is known as an irradiation illusion.

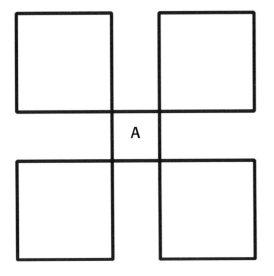

Which square is bigger, A or B?

Do you think the inner square (labeled B) inside the figure on the right is bigger? If so, your perception has been influenced by the small surrounding squares (this happens to most people). The small surrounding squares make the center appear bigger than it really is. In fact, squares A and B are of the same size.

Do you see a distorted hexagon?

If the six triangles were removed from this illustration, you could see that the hexagon underneath is perfect, and not distorted in any way. If you have doubts, take a ruler or pencil and trace the individual lines. The reason for the apparent distortion is that our mind projects the lines that run into the midpoint of the sides of the triangles to the center of the triangle, rather than continuing to the point where they meet each other.

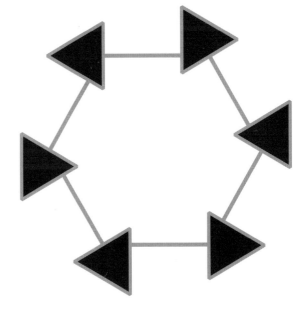

Which of the inner orange circles is bigger?

Most people overestimate the dimension of the right circle and believe it to be bigger than the one on the left. If you check their size with a ruler, though, you will find that both circles have the exact same diameter. This example illustrates how we perceive the size of objects depending on their context. The general rule is: the smaller the objects in the surroundings, the larger anything in the inner area appears.

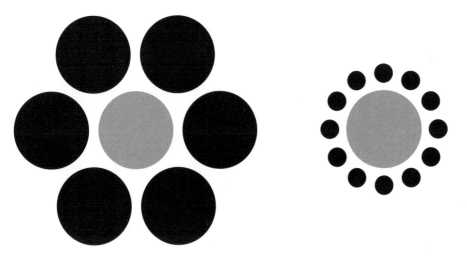

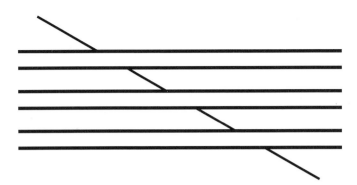

Is the diagonal line straight or jagged?

Although our impression tells us differently, the diagonal is a straight line. This optical illusion was recognized by German physicist Johann Christian Poggendorf in 1860 and has been named after him. While this is a particularly astonishing illusion that has received a lot of attention from researchers, it remains unclear even today what exactly causes it. Some scientists believe it is based on the human propensity to perceive acute angles as bigger and obtuse angles as smaller than they actually are. Perhaps this is what leads us to misjudge the angles of the diagonal line, and thus perceive the line as displaced.

Is this circle complete?

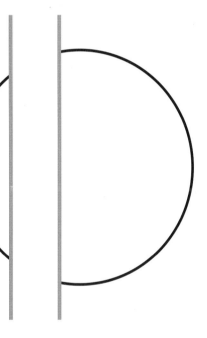

This illustration is an example of a variant of the Poggendorf illusion. The two vertical lines that intersect the circle lead us to believe that the circumference of the segment on the right would be greater than that of the segment on the left if the segments were continued. However, this is not the case: when the segments are extended, a perfect circle is formed.

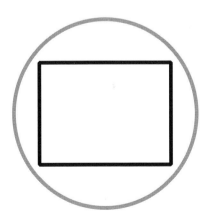

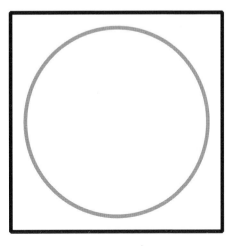

Which circle is smaller?

In tests, many people assume the left circle is the smaller one, but this is an illusion. In fact, both circles have the same diameter. The misperception is caused by the surrounding rectangle, which makes the surface area of the right circle appear bigger than it is. In the left circle with its inscribed rectangle, it is the other way around.

Giant car or tiny people?

Are you confused? Are you having trouble figuring out whether the car is very big and the two people in the background very small? If so, this car commercial was effective: the car does not actually exist. There are no hubcaps and tires, no headlights, no windshield and doors. Instead, what you can see here is a fascinating example of anamorphic painting. Employing extreme distortion techniques, pavement artists Edgar Müller, Manfred Stader, and Gregor Wosik have created an apparently three-dimensional object on the pavement. The perception of these illusions, however, depends on one's angle of vision: when seen from the side, the effect is lost.

Why are road markings elongated?

From a bird's-eye view, road markings such as the bicycle painted on bicycle lanes or the stop sign on a road appear exaggeratedly lengthened. When someone driving on the road approaches such a marking, however, it seems to be normally proportioned and is easily perceived. This kind of simple yet highly effective anamorphic representation is based on a road-user's normal angle of vision: typically, no bicycle rider or car driver has a bird's-eye view of the signs. This form of representation is also used for speed limits and arrows on the road.

Hans Holbein the Younger, *The Ambassadors* (1533), National Gallery, London.

Do you see anything unusual about this painting?

If you don't see it at first glance, change your angle of vision: tilt your head and focus on the area in the bottom left corner of the painting. Something unusual and unexpected emerges from the picture: a skull! This portrait of the two French envoys Jean de Dinteville and Georges de Selve is one of the oldest and most famous anamorphic paintings. It was created in 1533 by the Renaissance artist Hans Holbein the Younger. Today, it can be admired at the National Gallery in London.

Which objects on this road actually exist?

All kinds of things, but not the butterfly, the gaping chasm, and the cracks in the asphalt. This work of art was created during the Prairie Arts Festival in Canada, where both aspiring and established pavement artists come to demonstrate their skills. This giant butterfly hovering above a chasm was executed by Edgar Müller, one of the most famous pavement artists in the world. The flat picture on the road measures a whopping 23 ft x 39 ft! Anamorphic paintings on streets have become an increasingly popular advertising medium, and pavement art has thus acquired an entirely new significance.

Which side of the red rectangle is the longest?

All four sides are the same length! The impression of varying lengths is caused by the densely radiating lines on the right. The rectangle's right side is crossed by almost twice as many blue lines as the left side, which makes it appear to be longer. This illusion was first described by psychologist William Orbison in 1939, which is why it is called the Orbison illusion.

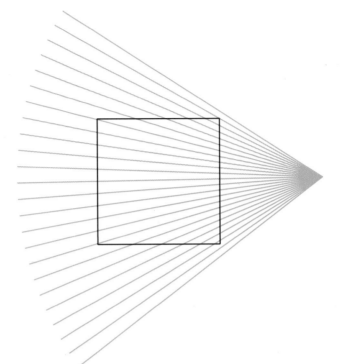

Which sides of the squares are curved?

Our perception may lead us to think differently, but in fact, not one of the sides of these squares is curved. In the diagram on the right, the four horizontal lines seem to be curved. In this case, the lines in the background intersect the sides of the squares at an obtuse angle, thus causing an optical illusion. In the diagram on the left, all four sides of the square seem to be distorted. Again, the illusion is caused by the circles in the background.

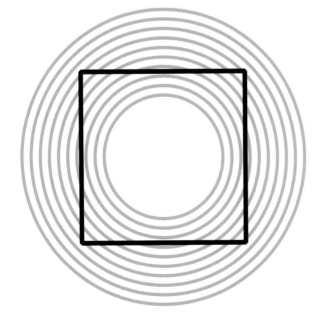
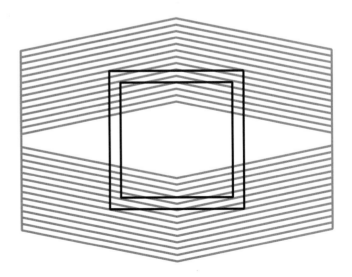

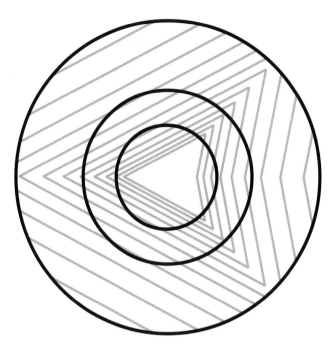

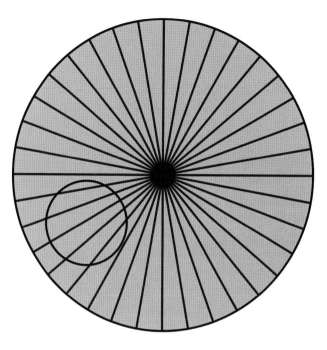

Which of these circles is most distorted?

Both of these geometric shapes provide further evidence that not only do we perceive squares as distorted when they are set against a background of lines in certain arrangements, but the same is also true of circles. Don't be deceived, though: in both cases, the shapes are in fact perfect circles!

Which lines in this sine curve are the longest?

The majority of people think that the lines are clearly the shortest in the gradient and that they grow longer in the curves, reaching their maximum length at the curves' turning points. In fact, both of these assumptions are wrong: the vertical lines are all of equal length.

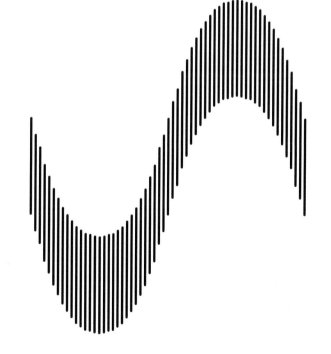

MOTION ILLUSIONS

A word of warning concerning the illustrations on the following pages is in order: your perception will be put to the test by things such as rotating circles and steam engines that appear to be moving. Two characteristics of the human perceptual system are mainly responsible for these kinds of illusions. First, visual perceptions create after-images on the retina that last for approximately 0.06 to 0.1 seconds. If images are presented to the eye in succession at a frequency of around 18 images per second, the individual images start to blend, thus creating the illusion of motion. This effect is the cause of a variety of illusions of motion, whether in cinema or in the illustrations on the following pages. Another cause of motion illusions lies in contrasts of color and brightness: the direction of the motion is determined by shifts in brightness (from black to white), causing fascinating tricks of the eye.

Rotating Snakes *is the title of one of the many fascinating works by Akiyoshi Kitaoka. Kitaoka, a professor of psychology at Ritsumeikan University in Japan, is one of the most important creators of illusions of motion.*

Which way around are the seahorses going?

This illustration of "dancing" seahorses, entitled *Rotating Seahorses*, is another work by Akiyoshi Kitaoka, a professor of psychology in Kyoto, Japan. The direction the animals are facing corresponds to the rotary motion of the circles: the group on the left rotates clockwise, while the right group rotates counter-clockwise.

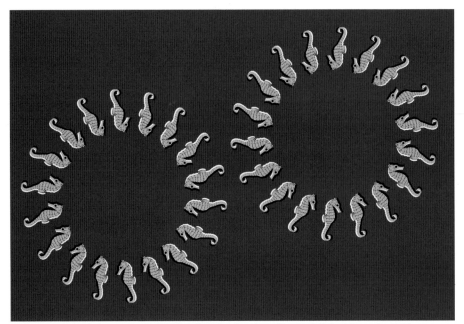

Seahorse © Akiyoshi Kitaoka 2003/© KANZEN This seahorse is a clipart image "Crust009" (© Corel Corporation 1997)

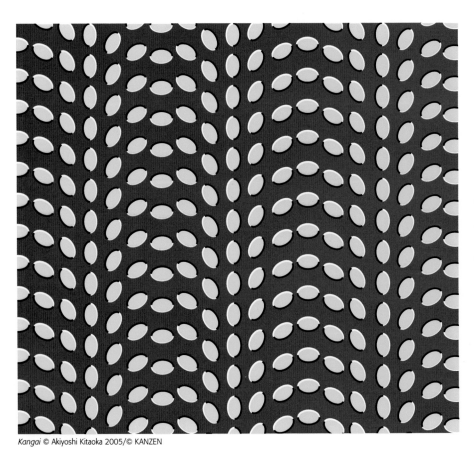

Kangai © Akiyoshi Kitaoka 2005/© KANZEN

Why are the yellow dots moving?

The somewhat jerky movements of our eye muscles cause the illusion of motion in this illustration, which is entitled *Kangai*. We can put a stop to the apparent rotation of the cylinder-like objects for a short amount of time if we focus on one spot without blinking. As soon as we move our eyelids, however, they continue to move. The picture symbolizes the motion of water in Japanese paddy-fields: *Kangai* means irrigation.

Are the letters dancing in front of your eyes?

No need to worry—it's just another work of art by Akiyoshi Kitaoka. This picture, which is entitled *ECVP waves*, makes the letters seem to move in a wave pattern. Kitaoka designed this picture for a contest on the occasion of ECVP, the European Conference on Visual Perception, which took place in 2005 in La Coruña, Spain. Among other things, scientists from all over the world also discussed the subject of optical illusions.

ECVPwavesstrong © Akiyoshi Kitaoka 2005/© KANZEN

Does it look as if the waves are moving?

If so, then everything is fine. Our eyes are in constant motion. In this example, afterimages of one portion of the image are still lingering on our retina while we are already processing the next part of the image. The overlap of these two visual impressions is what causes the illusion of movement.

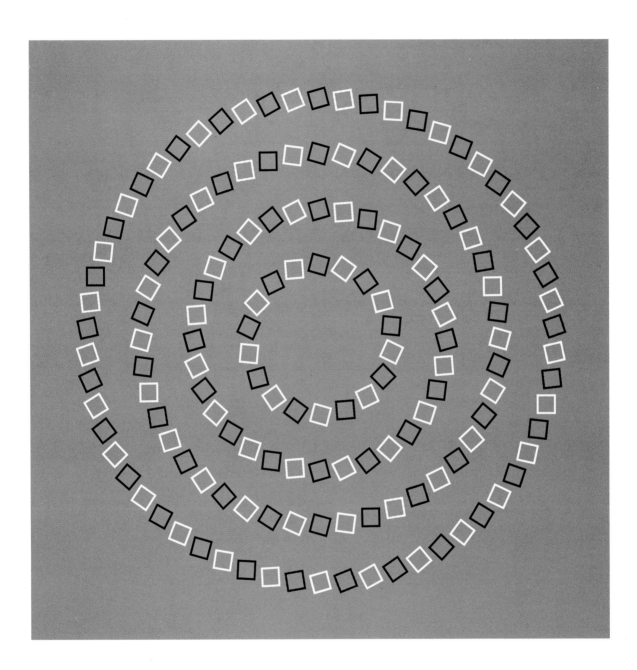

Move your head.
What is happening?

This visual illusion does not become apparent unless you tilt your head from side to side. As soon as you do, the circles begin to rotate. Moreover, there is an additional effect: it is hard to deter-mine whether the picture shows four individual circles or a rotating spiral. A considerable amount of concentration is required in order to even perceive the four separate circles.

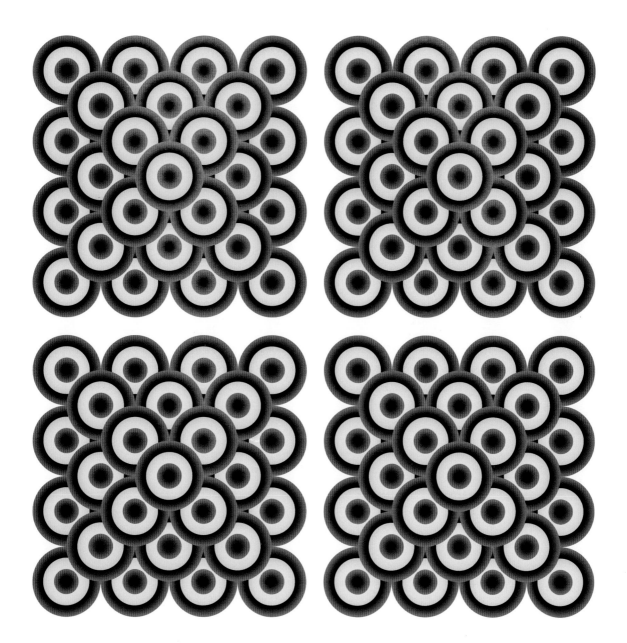

What motion do you perceive in this picture?

By now, there is nothing that Akiyoshi Kitaoka cannot set in motion. You don't even need to move your head or the image for his illusions to have their effect, as exemplified in this picture called *Purple tops*. The stacked circular objects seem to be continually expanding and pulsating—yet in reality, their surface does not change at all.

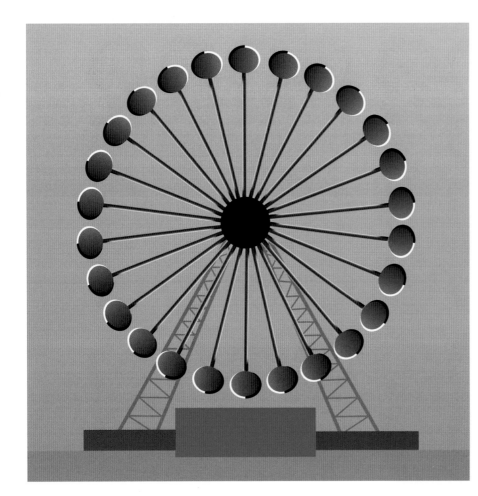

Can you set the Ferris wheel in motion?

Yes, you can! This Ferris wheel works without a motor and without animation. The impression of clockwise rotation is created solely by employing certain formal principles in creating the "cars." This picture was created by Herman Verwaal, a Dutch artist who specializes in illusions of motion.

Can robots come to life?

Presented with these two figures, who could deny it? While the circles that make up both figures have the same structure, they are aligned differently. The resulting transitions in contrast cause an optical illusion of the robots dancing in fluid, elegant motions.

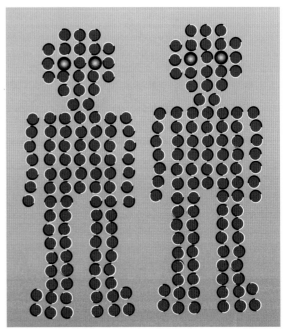

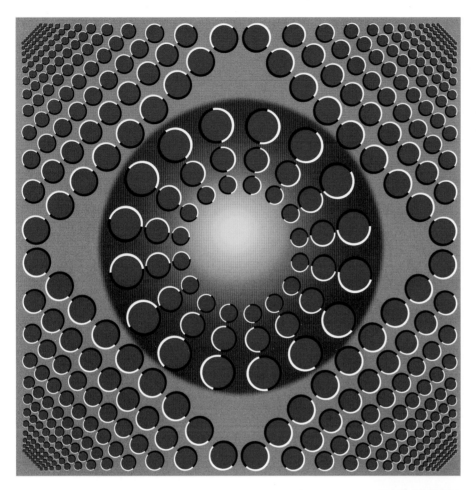

What's moving here and how?

This illusion of motion is most effective if you do not focus on the center, but look at the picture out of the corner of your eye. If you do so, the four fields with their strong effect of depth that mark the boundary of the inner shape seem to open up to reveal a clockwise-rotating figure.

How do red petals turn into green ones?

Focus on the circle in the center of the flower. You will soon be under the impression that the blue field surrounding it is expanding; the flower seems to be opening. Apart from this illusion of motion, this picture involves another illusion: if you stare at the image for a long time and then look at a white surface, you will notice a negative afterimage: the petals appear to be light green.

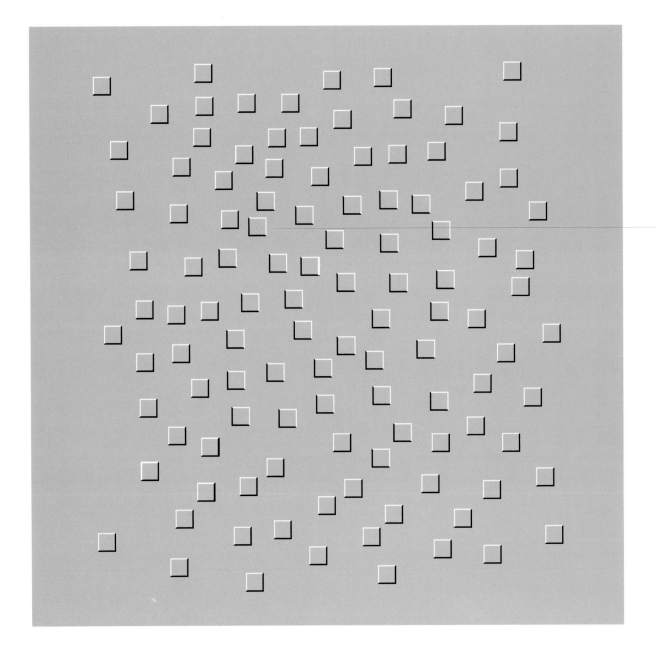

Can you move the squares?

Do you think that's not possible? Try moving your head back and forth a couple of times. After a while, the small squares start moving in different directions, and the distance between them seems to vary. If you focus on a particular point in the image, you will be able to stop some of the squares from moving; at the periphery, however, they will continue to move.

Do you see the rings moving?

If not, try to focus your attention on the black spot in the center of the picture. Then, slowly move your head first toward it, then away from it. The four rings seem to rotate in alternating directions. This visual illusion was developed by and named after Baingio Pinna. It is caused by an irritation of the nerve cells that are responsible for detecting the direction of motion of individual objects.

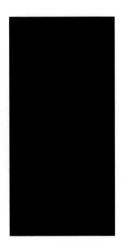

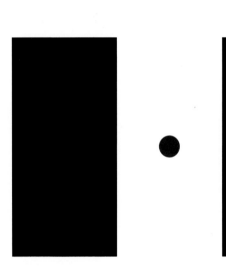

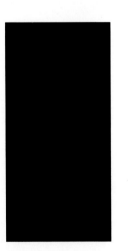

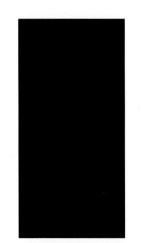

COLOR ILLUSIONS AND AFTERIMAGES

Everything is relative—this, in much abbreviated form, is the essence of Albert Einstein's highly complex theory of relativity, which teaches us that time, space, and motion are not absolute, but depend on the perspective of the observer. If something as seemingly clear as the phenomenon of speed cannot be established in absolute terms, though, how much more difficult must it be to determine size, color or shape? This chapter shows that our perception of things is not absolute. We can be deceived by illusions of contrast, which make us see things that don't really exist. Thus, an image may contain two or more lines, depending on the angle from which we look at it. Objects that seem to be clearly defined turn out to be constructions of our brains, and some remarkable examples make the point that colors are particularly hard to identify.

Create a negative afterimage by focusing on the red spot. After 30 seconds, look at a white surface. The black rectangles will appear bright while the white grid will turn dark.

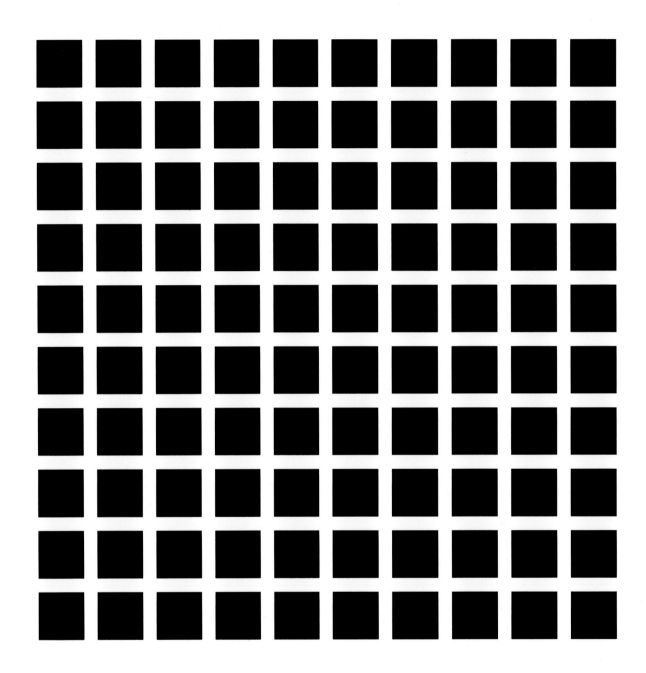

Do you notice anything special about this grid?

If you let your eyes wander over this grid, you will notice gray spots where the white lines cross. These spots, of course, do not actually exist. A German physiologist named Ludimar Hermann discovered this optical illusion, called lateral inhibition, which is based on antagonistic inhibition of receptors on the retina as well as on the fact that our eye compresses and encodes information which is subsequently misinterpreted by our brain.

Do you perceive light red spots in this grid?

Similarly, lateral inhibition causes an optical illusion in the case of this red-and-white pattern. Cells that are responsible for transmitting optical signals can be either inhibited or excited, depending on whether a light stimulus falls into the center or the periphery of the cell. In the areas where the lines intersect, the cells are inhibited. In the case of the illustration above, we perceive this effect as rapidly scintillating bright red spots.

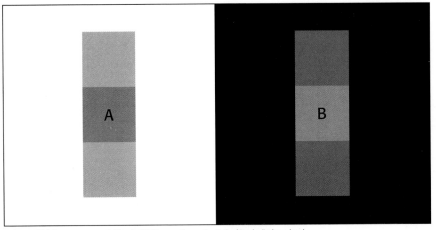

Enhanced brightness contrast © Kitaoka 2005 www.ritsumei.ac.jp/~akitaoka/index-e.html

Which field is brighter, A or B?

It probably seems to you that field B on the right is distinctly brighter than field A. In fact, the two fields have exactly the same hue. This image, *Enhanced Brightness Contrast*, illustrates that our perception of hue and brightness is relative: it clearly varies depending on the coloring of the surrounding areas.

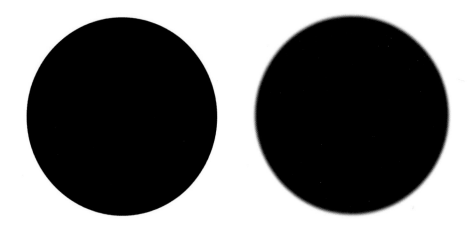

Are the two disks different in color?

Does the disk on the left appear to be darker than the one on the right? Rest assured, both shapes are identical with regard to hue and opacity. The illusion is caused by the difference in their sharpness. The left disk has a clearly delineated outline with high contrast, which makes it appear darker and fuller, while the opposite is true of the disk on the right.

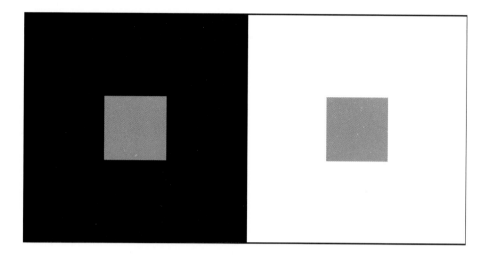

Do the gray squares have the same hue?

This is another example of how background colors influence our perception of color. The right square seems to be darker. The apparent difference in color is less striking, however, than in the top illustration on page 50. The reason for this lies in the absence of adjacent gray fields, which increased the effect of the illusion on the opposite page by adding other hues.

Which disk is darker?

Do you think that it is the one on the right? Most observers would say so. In this case, the lighter background is interpreted by our brain as a higher level of illumination of the object. Both disks reflect the same amount of light, yet the apparent difference in illumination makes the right disk appear darker. This effect is known as simultaneous brightness contrast.

Can you identify elements of the same color?

There seem to be several solutions, but hardly anyone would agree that the four small squares in the center of the picture belong together. In fact, they do have the same hue. In this case, the small size of the squares adds to the illusion of increased difference in brightness depending on surrounding areas.

Which of the four small squares have the same hue?

All four of them do! This example illustrates that in addition to perceived contrast in brightness, there also is a simultaneous contrast effect related to color.

Surfaces of the same color may be interpreted by our brains as being of varying colors if they are surrounded by differently colored contexts.

Do you see different shades of gray in this bar?

If so, try covering the entire background with a piece of paper. You will be surprised to see that the bar is actually uniformly colored in one shade of gray. The visual illusion, a case of simultaneous brightness contrast, is caused by the gradient of gray shades in the background. The bar appears lighter against a dark background, while a light background makes it appear to be darker.

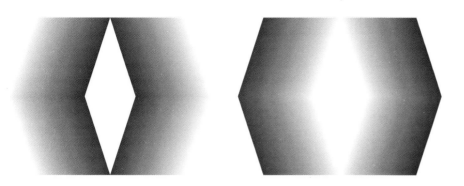

Which diamond has more luminance?

Despite the claims of washing detergent commercials, there is no such thing as "whiter than white." And yet that is exactly the impression we get from these illustrations. In fact, the figures are equally bright. But while there is a clear difference in contrast for the left shape, the background gradiant for the right diamond has been reversed. That is why this figure seems to be "whiter," even downright radiant.

Is the horizontal bar uniformly black?

You probably have the impression that the yellow stripes surrounding the black bar continue in the background, leaving an impression of color on the bar. But this illustration, created by Japanese psychologist Akiyoshi Kitaoka, is called a phototopic phantom for a reason. In fact, the bar is a homogenous black.

Receding color/Enhanced Fraser-Wilcox illusion, Type III and *photopic phantoms* © Kitaoka (2006) and Kitaoka, Gyoba and Kawabata (1999)

What shapes are in the spaces at the ends of the black lines?

The answer is deceptively simple: white circles. But do these white circles really exist? No, they don't! The clearly delineated, full circles we perceive are a visual illusion. Furthermore, these phantom circles seem to be distinctly brighter than the white background, almost as if they were shining. This variant of the Hermann grid was developed by Walter Ehrenstein.

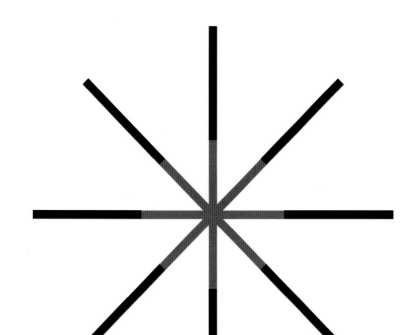

What do you perceive where the lines meet?

This illustration represents a modification of the Ehrenstein illusion on the opposite page. In this case, there are no gaps masking the intersection of the lines. Instead, a smaller red star is superimposed on the large black star, which makes us perceive a light red circle whose circumference is determined by the length of the red lines.

Does the disk in the center of the picture appear to be "whiter than white"?

This question should be answered with another question: "What disk?" As in the Ehrenstein figure on the previous page, there is no disk where the lines intersect—the disk we perceive is an illusion. The contrast illusions involved here have not yet been fully explained, but they make the phantom disk appear whiter than its background.

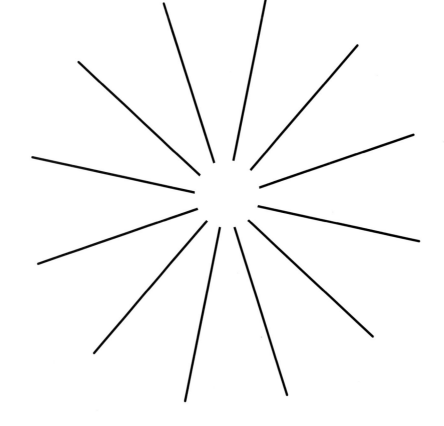

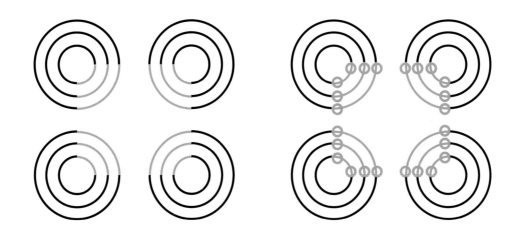

Do you see a turquoise square in this picture?

The left illustration creates an illusion of a semi-transparent, turquoise square that has been superimposed on segments of the circles and part of the background. In fact, the turquoise color is limited to a quarter of each circumference. As the illustration on the right shows, this illusion of color—which is based on an effect known as neon color spreading—is lost when the small circles are added. They interfere with the interpreting process of our brain.

Do you notice anything special about the white squares in this grid?

If you compare the hues of the tiny squares at the intersections of the black lines with the white background of the grid, the tiny squares will appear brighter and more radiant. This figure is an inverted variant of the Hermann grid. In this case, the relevant receptors are not inhibited but excited, causing the illusion that the squares on the grid are "whiter than white."

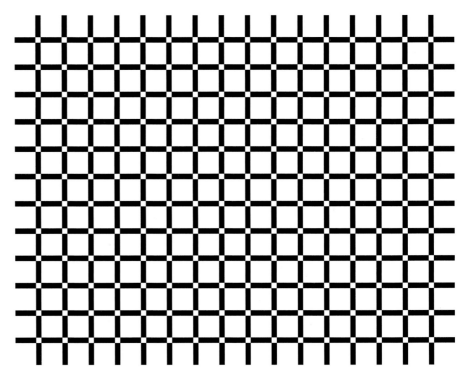

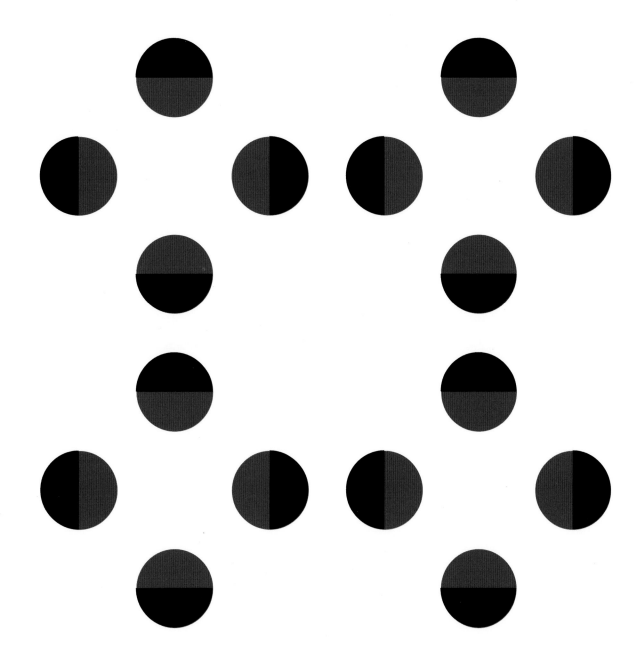

Photopic phantoms © Kitaoka, Gyoba and Kawabata (1999)

What can you see in this image apart from the black and blue disks?

In addition to the sixteen disks arranged in groups of four, a neon color illusion leads us to perceive four squares located in the center of the groups. The effect is quite striking: four colored half-disks aligned to face each other generate an illusion of a clearly delineated rectangle, which the human brain automatically fills in with a color.

Do you see two lines or three in this figure?

Don't be too quick with your answer: while you may be convinced that there are only two lines, a change in perspective will make you reconsider. Try looking at the image not from above, but from below the edge of the page. Move it close to your eyes: you will be surprised to see that a third line appears.

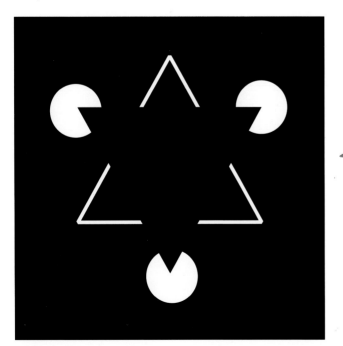

Can you see the triangles in these two diagrams?

These are Kanisza triangles (developed by Gaetano Kanisza), an impressive demonstration of our brain's natural tendency to fill in incomplete images to create whole shapes. Each of the forms contains a triangle that seems to hover in the foreground and that is perceived as being "whiter than white" or "blacker than black" as the result of a contrast illusion.

What do you perceive in this picture?

A single glance is enough for us to pick out a Christmas tree. Even when we rotate the picture or cover part of it, this apparently meaningless constellation of partially cut-out black disks is filled in and interpreted as a coherent whole by our brain. Not only are the disks arranged in our perception to form a fir tree, they even provide the holiday decoration for it, as well.

How many triangles do you see in this picture?

The typical answer is two. This variant of a Kanisza triangle illustrates just how few clues our brain actually requires in order for it to recognize familiar shapes: three red dots are enough to create a perfect illusion of a triangle with no real outlines. We rely on this cognitive capacity to complete shapes for orientation in everyday life.

How can this green heart be made red without paint or crayons?

Quite simply—if not on paper, then with your inner eye. To do this, stare fixedly at the image for about 30 seconds, and then look at a white surface. You will see a red heart. This phenomenon is known as a negative afterimage, and is caused by the fatigue (or loss of sensitivity) of the receptor cells located on the retina.

What afterimage is created by this pattern?

Look at this picture for approximately 30 seconds before looking at a white surface. The fields that are red in the original picture change into a radiant blue, the complementary color of red. Strong afterimage effects are among the reasons why staff in operating rooms tend to wear blue or green scrubs: staring at open wounds for an extended period of time would cause irritating blue afterimages on white sheets and garments.

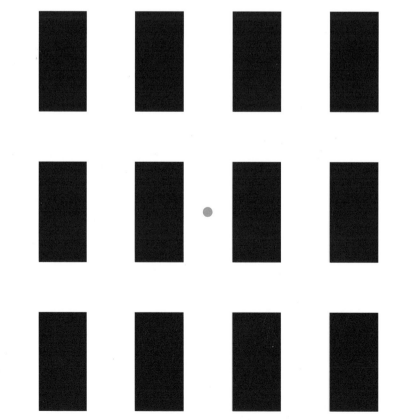

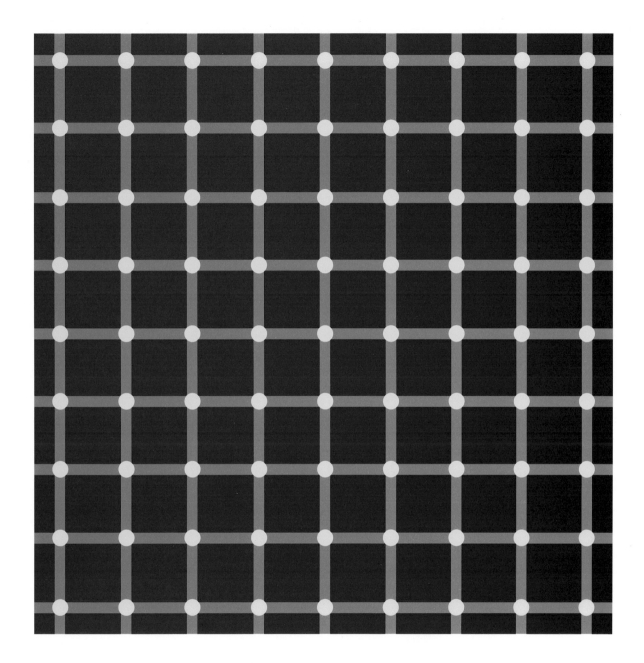

Can you count the blue and yellow spots where the lines cross?

Try as you may, it is impossible: the scintillating blue spots vanish the moment you try to focus on them. This visual illusion was discovered in 1994 by Elke Lingelbach while she was trying to program variants of the Hermann grid illusion. The cause of this stunning illusion is not yet understood.

AMBIGUOUS PATTERNS AND PUZZLE PICTURES

Have you ever wondered how humans actually perceive things in three dimensions? This ability, which we take for granted, relies on a highly complex process. Our perception of the three-dimensional world is, in fact, based on a two-dimensional representation on the retina of the eye, which has to be decoded and reconstructed in three-dimensional terms by our brain. This process sometimes leaves more than one interpretation open, as is illustrated by the puzzle pictures in this chapter. There are a range of fascinating images that allow for more than one possible interpretation: whether you see a candle or two faces in profile, a frog or a horse, one or several shapes—there is no single "right" or "wrong," but a number of valid perceptual variations.

In this 16th-century work by Giuseppe Arcimboldo, various kitchen utensils are combined into one highly interesting figure.

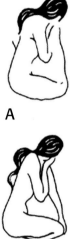

A

B

A man's face or a woman?

If you look at these eight drawings one after another, the man's face gradually turns into a seated woman. Interestingly, in tests, people who are shown only the top row do not pick out the figure of a woman in image A. Conversely, when presented with only the bottom row of figures, they do not see a man's face in image B, even though the two drawings are almost identical. This illustrates how the interpretation of a picture is dependent on contextual information.

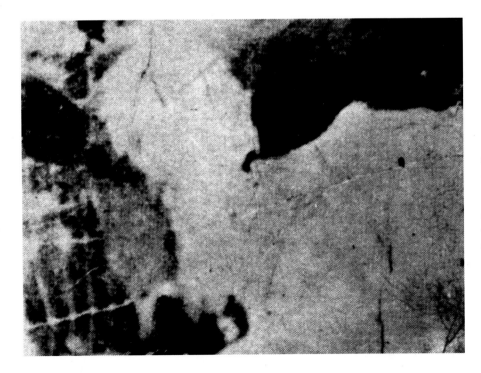

Can you see an animal in this picture?

Once you spot the animal hidden in these black-and-white shapes, it is hard to see how you could have missed it (it is a cow). The cow's head fills the left half of the picture, the black patches in the lower area represent its nose and mouth, and further up there are additional black areas for its eyes and ears.

Everyone sees the cat, but where is the mouse?

The cat may well appreciate the answer: the mouse is right in its face. The rodent's ears correspond to the cat's eyes, the eyes to the cat's nose, and both animals share one and the same mouth. What a clever way to hide!

Apart from the frog, another animal is hiding in this picture. Where is it?

To see the second animal, rotate the image 90° counterclockwise. You will instantly identify the form of a horse's head. Once we have discovered the horse, our perception oscillates between frog and horse even when the picture is viewed from the original angle.

Where do the camels come from?

A flip book or an animated cartoon of this sequence would require a great many pictures; here, the same effect is condensed into a single illustration. Looking at it from left to right, the spaces in between the palm trees become camels. This transformation is achieved with only a few modifications—yet the transition is not abrupt, but continuous and smooth.

Octavio Ocampo, *Kalvarienberg*

Do you notice anything special about this painting?

First, look at the image from a distance. It seems to be a painting of Jesus on the cross, the kind that might be found in countless churches. Upon closer inspection, however, this painting that appears to be so homogeneous when seen from a distance turns out to be composed out of many smaller pictures, all of which are related to the subject of the crucifixion.

Sandro Del-Prete, *Don Quijote*

What do you see in this picture?

This is a painting by Swiss artist Sandro Del-Prete, who has created a series of pictures he refers to as "illusorisms." It is a portrait of Don Quixote, the tragic hero who famously fought the windmills in Miguel de Cervantes' early seventeenth-century novel of the same title. Don Quixote's right eye, nose, mouth, and beard represent the hero as a whole, sitting astride Rocinante, his "war-horse." The windmills can be seen in the background.

Octavio Ocampo, *The General's Family* (1990)

How many faces are there in this painting?

At first glance, this painting by Octavio Ocampo seems to show only the face of a bearded old man in profile. On closer inspection, however, one realizes that the front of the face also represents a man wearing a hat and carrying a walking stick, while the back part of the old man's head reveals a woman holding a baby. Also, take a good look at the coping of the wall: it contains another four faces in profile and one seen from the front.

Salvador Dalí, *Disappearing Bust of Voltaire* (1941), Salvador Dalí Museum, St. Petersburg, Florida

The bust of a famous philosopher is hidden in this illustration. Where? Who is it?

Focus on the left half of the image. The left arch forms the cranium, the faces of the two people walking through the arch are the eyes, and parts of their bodies correspond to the nose, mouth, and chin of . . . Voltaire, the great Enlightenment philosopher. The creator of this painting is no less famous: Salvador Dalí, one of the most famous representatives of surrealism.

Giuseppe Arcimboldo, *Summer* (ca. 1580), Brescia

What does this collection of fruits and vegetables represent?

This is not merely a random arrangement of fruits and vegetables, but an inspired composition of the shape of a woman. She is half recumbent, leaning against the wall, wearing a hat and looking to the right. This painting was done in the sixteenth century by the Italian painter Giuseppe Arcimboldo.

Salvador Dalí, *Swans Reflecting Elephants* (1937), private collection

What animals have been immortalized in this painting by Salvador Dalí?

This painting from 1937 is the artistic application of a "discovery" Dalí had made while watching swans on a lake: a swan's reflection in the water has a striking resemblance to the head of an elephant. Thus, the reflection of the three swans in the center of the picture reveals three elephants.

Octavio Ocampo, *Portrait of Francisco I. Madero* (1980), Celaya

What is hidden in this portrait?

This mural by Celayan native Octavio Ocampo is located in the town hall of Celaya, Mexico. It represents one of the three protagonists of the Mexican Revolution. The big portrait shows Francisco I. Madero, who proclaimed the revolution in 1910. His head is formed with five skilfully arranged figures. His jacket simultaneously represents the Mexican flag, and the flowers and foliage in the picture form the men's garments.

Giuseppe Arcimboldo, *Spring* (1589), Louvre, Paris

An arrangement of flowers or a woman's face?

It is both at the same time! By skillfully arranging flowers and foliage, Guiseppe Arcimboldo has created a somewhat ambiguous painting. Looking at the picture from a distance, we recognize a woman wearing a flower arrangement on her head. On closer inspection, though, we realize that her face is composed of petals and leaves down to the most minute detail.

What figures are hidden in this Dalí painting?

At first glance we perceive mountains, a sandy terrain, several people, and four fires. However, each of the three persons in the center of the painting form part of a portrait of Spanish writer Frederico García Lorca. Following the smoke of the fires upward, we are surprised to find that the smoke turns into a giant white dog, an Afghan.

Salvador Dalí, *Invisible Afghan* (1938), private collection

Where has Salvador Dalí depicted the *Metamorphosis of Narcissus*?

In the left half of the painting, at the shores of the lake, there is a figure of a crouching man. This figure represents Narcissus, a character from Greek mythology. Narcissus fell in love with his own reflection in a pool formed by a spring. Incapable of tearing himself away from it, he eventually died at the spring and was transformed into a narcissus flower (which can also be seen in the painting).

Salvador Dalí, *Metamorphosis of Narcissus* (1937), Tate Gallery, London

Charles Allan Gilbert, *All is Vanity* (1892)

Is there anything uncanny about this painting?

If you don't see anything particularly frightening, take a closer look at the mirror: its outline forms a skull, with the woman's head and its reflection representing the eye sockets. Once discovered, this secret also gives additional import to the sentence at the bottom of the painting: *All is Vanity*.

Popular Print, *Napoleon at his Grave*, UK 1831 (pub. R. Ackermann)

Can you see Napoleon in this picture?

At first glance, this picture seems to represent no more than a memorial slab with some trees on a beach in the background. However, if you take a closer look at the space between the trees, you will see the silhouette of Napoleon wearing his famous cocked hat. The figure is formed by the trunks of the trees. Napoleon's arms are crossed, and he is looking at his own grave.

Can you see Jacques and Jack?

No? Take a closer look at the maple leaf in the Canadian flag: you will notice two faces in profile. Their long noses are formed by the indentations of the leaf in the upper left and right corners. In reference to the two official languages in Canada, these figures are known among Canadians as Jacques and Jack.

What do you see in this illustration?

This image is a good example of how ambiguous representations make it impossible for us to commit to a single interpretation. Instead, our perception keeps alternating. In this case, we are able to alternately see either a white candle or the silhouettes of two faces in profile.

Octavio Ocampo, *Lupe* (1982)

How many people can be seen in this painting?

This painting is an impressive example of how homogenous an ambiguous, multi-layered picture can appear if they are viewed from a distance. Only when we take a closer look do we realize that the face of this black-haired woman is composed of a dancer and two male figures.

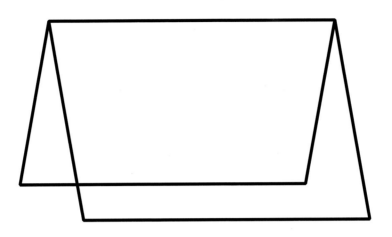

Which side of this figure is in the front?

A brief glance at this drawing seems to be sufficient to answer this question. But beware! If we keep looking at the picture, the figure suddenly shifts: the area that was initially at the back now seems to be in front. This change in perspective occurs involuntarily at first: the observer has no control over the perception. After a while, however, the effect becomes controllable.

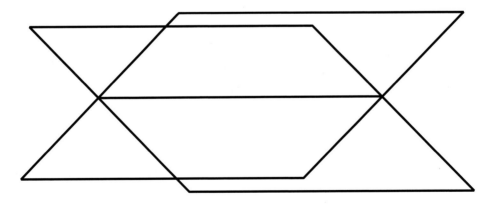

Look at this figure. Can you change perspectives at will?

This illustration is another example of a puzzle picture: two alternative narrow planes can be in the foreground. Our brains offer us several ways of interpreting the visual information. While this cognitive feature may lead to confusing results at times when looking at motionless objects, the capacity of "multistable perception" is very important for our orientation in everyday life.

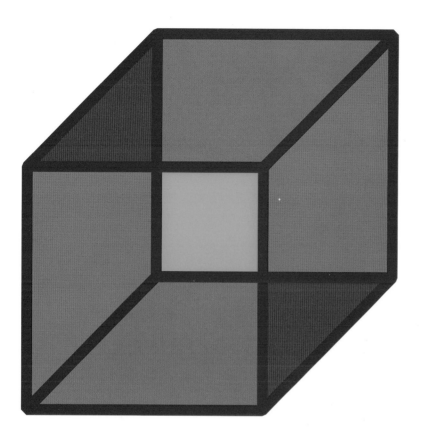

Which side of the cube is in the foreground?

This is a Necker cube, one of the best-known puzzle pictures. Again, two perceptual alternatives are available for interpreting this figure in three-dimensional space. It cannot be established which side of the cube is toward the front and which to the back: the sides shift continually.

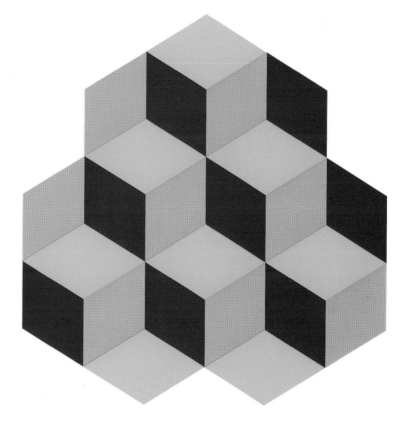

How many cubes can you see?

That depends on how you look at them: you can interpret the turquoise sides as either the top or the bottom surfaces. Depending on the interpretation you choose, you will count either six or seven cubes in this image.

IMPOSSIBLE OBJECTS AND IMAGES

Are you a firm believer in the irrefutable laws of physics, mathematics and geometry? Are you convinced that every object has a top and a bottom, that all stairs have to lead somewhere, and that the sum of the interior angles of a triangle always equals 180°? The following examples may well convince you otherwise. Famous artists such as M. C. Escher, István Orosz, Sandro Del-Prete, and Oscar Reutersvärd have all created pictures and objects that shake the very foundations of our convictions. In some cases, nothing appears to be amiss at first glance. On closer inspection, however, we find more and more elements that seem to defy the laws of nature. Art has the ability to represent what cannot exist in reality: it reveals an impossible and stunning world.

David MacDonald, *Impossible Terrace* (1999)

This is a structure that could not possibly exist in reality. In the upper half of this painting by David MacDonald, the terrace appears as seen from below; the lower half shows the terrace as seen from a bird's-eye view.

István Orosz, *Stairs* (2000)

What is wrong with this picture?

This painting by Hungarian artist István Orosz contains a number of oddities. Look at the stairs in the foreground: two people are on the stairs, both facing the same direction—yet one of them is walking down the stairs, the other is climbing up. How is this possible? And what about the light area in the upper section of the picture? Is it a wall? Is it a floor? Nothing in this picture can be identified with certainty—everything is a matter of perspective. Emphasizing the strangeness of it all, Orosz has mixed the styles of clothing worn by people in the picture: some are dressed in historic attire, while others wear contemporary clothes. The whole painting is a puzzling play on space and time.

Which side of this triangle is the exterior and which is the interior?

A simple law of geometry tells us that the sum of the angles in a triangle equals 180°, yet Penrose triangles like this one violate that law: all three sides of the shape are perpendicular to each other. The special arrangement of the individual elements makes it impossible for us to determine which sides are on the inside and which on the outside.

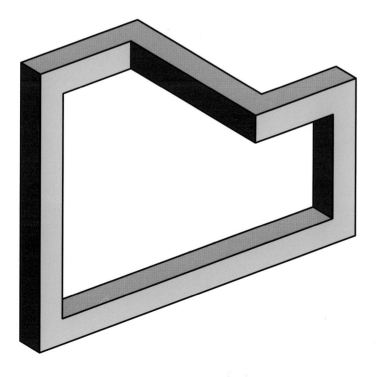

Why is this an impossible figure?

This is another object that violates the laws of geometry. If the top piece of this object is horizontal to the ground and does not slope, the structure cannot be closed if the vertical pieces are of different heights. The left side, however, appears to be significantly higher than the right one.

Why can this colonnade not be built in real life?

Indisputably, this picture shows three capitals forming the crown of three columns. However, when we try to follow the middle column from top to bottom, we realize that it disappears into nothingness. This is an interesting variant of the "devil's pitchfork" illustrated on page 87.

Who is going up the stairs and who is going down?

This picture shows an impossible staircase. Experience tells us that if two people encounter each other on stairs, one of them must be walking downward and the other upward. This knowledge is challenged here: both of the figures are going downstairs.

Why is the ball wider at the bottom than at the top?

This effect is caused by differences in the refraction of light. When light rays hit an object, they are reflected and hit the retina. However, light rays may also be deflected when they hit materials of different optical densities. In this example, the light that hits the upper half of the ball is reflected differently than the light that hits the lower half; light rays are refracted differently by air and water, respectively.

Shigeo Fukuda, *Disappearing Column*

Why is this object known as the "devil's pitchfork"?

At first, we seem to recognize a regular, three-pronged object. But we quickly wonder where the middle rod actually comes from. After all, only two of the prongs originate in the bar on the figure's short end. Did the devil perhaps have a hand in it?

Is it possible to tie this knot?

At first glance, this looks like a fairly realistic knot. However, let your eyes try to follow the rope from one end to the other. You will realize that it is not possible: at a certain point, you will lose track of it.

Are all the elephant's legs firmly on the ground?

Hardly—in fact, how many legs is it standing on, anyway? This "impossible elephant" was created by American psychologist Roger N. Shepard. The confusing thing about this picture is that we can unambiguously determine the number of the elephant's feet as four, yet we cannot count the number of its legs with certainty.

Roger Shepard, *Impossible Elephant*

István Orosz, *Pergola* (1993)

Would you enjoy sitting in this pergola?

The scenery may be picturesque and quite inviting, yet the construction of the columns should make you wonder. There's nothing special about the two columns on the outside, but the other four are very odd: instead of running straight up to the cupola, they meet the opposite side of the roof. A bold construction, indeed, and not only in terms of statics!

David MacDonald, *Peregrination*

Do you notice anything unusual about this building?

This picture contains a number of vertical components such as ladders, a block and tackle, columns, and other such things that all seem to be related to a staggered terrace construction. However, if you let your eyes follow the construction from the bottom of the picture to the top, which seems to be at a higher level, you will realize that in fact there is no difference in altitude. This fascinating image is a smorgasbord of perspectival impossibilities!

Could this object actually be constructed?

The answer is no: the vertical line in the background crosses a horizontal line in the foreground. Looking at the picture a little longer, though, you will realize that this impossible object is at the same time also a puzzle picture like those presented in the chapter on puzzle pictures: two possible front planes alternately switch to the foreground.

Could these blocks of wood be arranged like this in real life?

The impossibility of this arrangement is revealed on inspection of the outer elements: on the left side, two blocks are arranged vertically, yet on the right, the blocks are transposed, almost adjacent to each other. Since each of the elements has the same height, the outer blocks on the left side would have to be arranged similarly to the outer blocks on the right side.

Does this garden gate open toward the inside or the outside?

The hinges on the pillars suggest that the gate opens to the outside. Upon closer inspection of the two gates, however, we realize that it is impossible to determine which way they open. This example of an impossible object was created by Dutch artist Herman Verwaal, who has also created a wide range of illusions of motion.

Could you sit on this chair and at this table?

Even if this table and chair drawn by Herman Verwaal could be built in real life, we shudder to think of trying to use them! Aside from the problem that they probably would not be very stable, the real issue is the fact that we cannot tell where the tops and bottoms of the seat and the tabletop are.

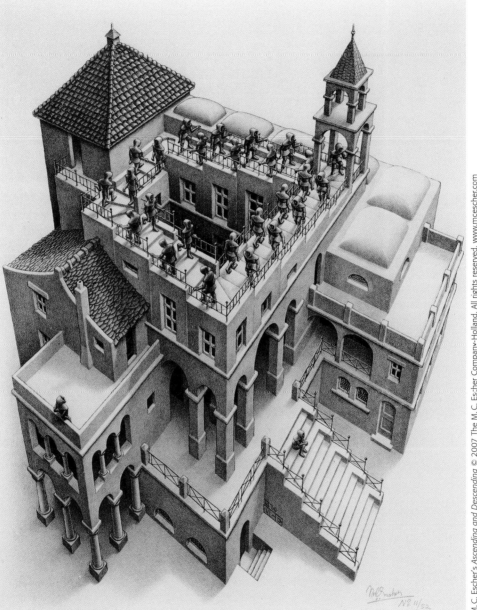

Can the people on the stairs ever reach their destination?

Ascending and Descending—this is the thematic title of one of the best known pictures by Dutch artist M. C. Escher. Many of his works of art deal with perspective impossibilities and multistable constructs, as illustrated by this drawing. No matter whether the people on the stairs are ascending or descending, they can never make any real progress: all of them are trapped in an endless cycle of stairs that ultimately lead nowhere.

Why are there no streams like this in real life?

Waterfall is another of M. C. Escher's famous works that represents an impossible construction. The center of the drawing shows a waterfall that drives a mill-wheel—there is nothing impossible about this. But follow the stream: it is flowing downward, away from the observer. Consequently, the most distant point would have to be the lowest point of the stream. Instead, this is actually the highest point, from which the water falls down all over again.

Further Reading

Block, J. Richard and Yuker, Harold. *Can You Believe Your Eyes?* Oxford: Routledge, 1989.

Hollmann, E. and Tesch, J. *A Trick of the Eye: Trompe L'oeil Masterpieces.* Munich, Berlin, London, New York, 2004.

Kitaoka, A. *Trick Eyes.* New York, 2005.

Kitaoka, A. *Trick Eyes Graphics.* Tokyo, 2005.

Ninio, Jacques. Transl Franklin Philip. *The Science of Illusions.* Ithaca, NY: Cornell Univ. Press, 2001.

Rodgers, Nigel. *Incredible Optical Illusions.* New York: Simon & Schuster, 1998.

Seckel, Al. *More Optical Illusions.* London: Carlton Books, 2002.

—— *The Art of Optical Illusions.* London: Carlton Books, 2000.

—— *SuperVisions: Ambiguous Optical Illusions.* New York: Sterling, 2005.

Seckel, Al and Hofstadter, Douglas. *Masters of Deception.* New York: Sterling, 2007.

Sturgis, Alexander. *Optical Illusions in Art.* London: Carlton Books, 2002.

Picture credits

Fabio Rieti, a painter and façade designer, working on a trompe-l'œil *in Paris.*

Page 96: While this looks like a daring jump over the young girl sleeping in the stroller, there is actually ample distance between them. Track competition in Atlanta, Georgia, 1952.